Melissa Stewart

Seals, Sea Lions, and Walruses

Franklin Watts - A Division of Scholastic Inc.
New York • Toronto • London • Auckland • Sydney
Mexico City • New Delhi • Hong Kong
Danbury, Connecticut

Photographs ©: Minden Pictures: 41 (Matthias Breiter), 1, 6, 15, 33 (Tui De Roy), 17 (Gerry Ellis), 19 (Michio Hoshino), 21 (Mitsuaki Iwago), 31, 42 bottom (Frans Lanting), 25 (Flip Nicklin), 13 (Konrad Wothe); Peter Arnold Inc.: 5 top left, 7 top, 37 (Fred Bruemmer); Photo Researchers: 29 (Tim Davis), 5 bottom right (Dan Guravich), 27 (Robert W. Hernandez), 43 (Tom & Pat Leeson), 42 top (Norman R. Lightfoot), 23 (C.K. Lorenz), 5 bottom left (Al Lowry), 5 top right, 7 bottom (Yva Momatiuk & John Eastcott), 39 (Terry Whittaker), cover, 35 (Art Wolfe).

Illustrations by José Gonzales and Steve Savage

The photo on the cover shows a harbor seal.
The photo on the title page shows a female Hooker's sea lion and her pup.

Visit Franklin Watts on the Internet at:
http://publishing.grolier.com

Library of Congress Cataloging-in-Publication Data

Stewart, Melissa.
Seals, sea lions, and walruses / Melissa Stewart; [illustrations by José Gonzalez and Steve Savage].
        p. cm. — (Animals in order)
    Includes bibliographical references and index.
    ISBN 0-531-11887-8 (lib. bdg.)
        1. Pinnipedia—Juvenile literature. [1. Pinnipeds.] I. Gonzales, José, ill. II. Savage, Steve, 1965– ill. III. Title. IV. Series.
QL737.P6 S73 2001
599.79—dc21   00-032514

GROLIER
PUBLISHING   1 2 3 4 5 6 7 8 9 10 R 10 09 08 07 06 05 04 03 02 01

Contents

What Is a Pinniped?

Can you think of some animals that live in the ocean? There are sharks and sea turtles, sardines and squid, shrimp and sea horses—to name just a few. The ocean is also the home of many *mammals*. Mammals have a backbone and drink their mothers' milk when they are young. Humans are mammals, and so are mice, cats, bears, and elephants.

Mammals that live in the ocean are called marine mammals. Whales, dolphins, manatees, and sea otters are all marine mammals. These animals have special body parts that help them live in salt water. Seals, sea lions, and walruses are marine mammals too. They belong to a group of animals called the *pinnipeds*. The word "pinniped" means "feather-footed."

The four animals shown on the next page are pinnipeds. Can you tell what they all have in common?

Harp seal

Northern fur seal

California sea lion

Walrus

Traits of Pinnipeds

While whales and dolphins spend all their time in the water, pinnipeds divide their time between the ocean and the land. During some parts of the year, pinnipeds spend most of their time in the water searching for fish, squid, and a variety of small ocean creatures. When it is time for pinnipeds to give birth to their young, choose a mate, or shed their old coat and grow a new one, they head for solid ground or ice.

A Galapagos fur seal

Seals, sea lions, and walruses are powerful swimmers and excellent divers. People can dive only about 30 feet (9 m) unless they are wearing special equipment. Some pinnipeds can dive as deep as 2,950 feet (899 m) and stay underwater for more than 2 hours.

Before a pinniped dives, it closes its nostrils and ears so no water can leak in. It empties its lungs and holds all the *oxygen* it needs in its blood and muscles. A pinniped also slows its heart rate and reduces the amount of blood that flows to some parts of its body.

A pinniped's blubber helps it stay warm in the chilly ocean water. The thick layer of oily fat also acts as a built-in energy supply. This is important because many pinnipeds go for long periods of time without eating. During the *breeding season*, a male pinniped may not eat for 3 months. Can you imagine going that long without food?

Antarctic fur seals fighting

Most pinnipeds spend part of the year living in large groups. They come together first to breed and then to *molt*. At the beginning of the breeding season, males usually move onto land first and fight for mating *territories*. A few weeks later, females arrive and give birth to pups. A pinniped mother spends the next few days nursing her baby with nutritious milk that she makes inside her body.

Some females feed their pups for just a few days. Then they choose a male, mate with him, and head out to sea for weeks. Other females nurse their pups for several months, but during that period, they spend some time at sea feeding themselves.

A few weeks or months after the breeding season is over, the adults return to land to molt. When the pinnipeds' new coats have grown in, they go back to the ocean. They spend most of their time swimming and feeding until the next breeding season.

Northern fur seals live in large groups while they molt.

The Order of Living Things

A tiger has more in common with a house cat than with a daisy. A true bug is more like a butterfly than a jellyfish. Scientists arrange living things into groups based on how they look and how they act. A tiger and a house cat belong to the same group, but a daisy belongs to a different group.

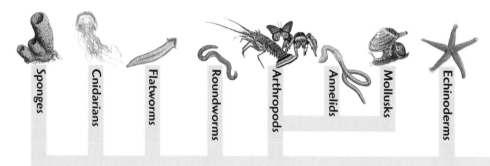

Sponges · Cnidarians · Flatworms · Roundworms · Arthropods · Annelids · Mollusks · Echinoderms

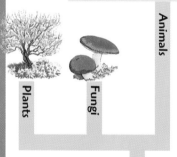

Animals

Plants · Fungi

Protists

Monerans

All living things belong to one of five groups called *kingdoms*: the plant kingdom, the animal kingdom, the fungus kingdom, the moneran kingdom, or the protist kingdom. You can probably name many of the creatures in the plant and animal kingdoms. The fungus kingdom includes mushrooms, yeasts, and molds. The moneran and protist kingdoms contain thousands of living things that are too small to see without a microscope.

8

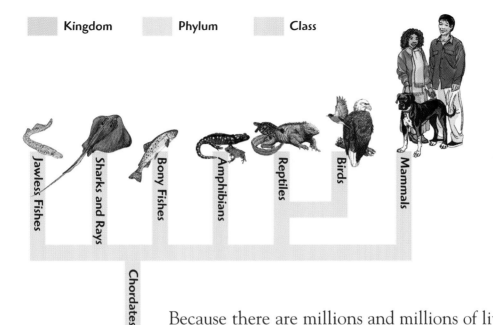

Kingdom Phylum Class

Jawless Fishes
Sharks and Rays
Bony Fishes
Amphibians
Reptiles
Birds
Mammals

Chordates

Because there are millions and millions of living things on Earth, some of the members of one kingdom may not seem all that similar. The animal kingdom includes creatures as different as tarantulas and trout, jellyfish and jaguars, salamanders and sparrows, elephants and earthworms.

To show that an elephant is more like a jaguar than an earthworm, scientists further separate the creatures in each kingdom into more specific groups. The animal kingdom is divided into nine *phyla*. Humans belong to the chordate phylum. All chordates have a backbone.

Each phylum can be subdivided into many *classes*. Humans, mice, and elephants all belong to the mammal class. Each class can be further divided into *orders*; orders into *families*, families into *genera*, and genera into *species*. All the members of a species are very similar.

9

How Pinnipeds Fit In

You can probably guess that pinnipeds belong to the animal kingdom. They have much more in common with snakes and squirrels than with maple trees and morning glories.

Pinnipeds belong to the chordate phylum. Almost all chordates have a backbone and a skeleton. Can you think of other chordates? Examples include raccoons, rabbits, alligators, frogs, birds, and fish. The chordate phylum can be divided into a number of classes. As you learned earlier, pinnipeds belong to the mammal class.

There are eighteen different orders of mammals. The pinnipeds make up one of these orders. Scientists divide the pinnipeds into three family groups: the walruses, the eared seals, and the true seals. There is only one species in the walrus family. A walrus's long tusks make it easy to recognize.

Eared seals have small flaps of skin over their ear holes and can waddle or gallop on land. In the water, they use their front flippers to propel themselves forward and their back flippers to steer. This group includes eight species of fur seals and five species of sea lions.

True seals do not have flaps of skin over their ear holes and cannot walk on land. They spend more time in the water and can dive deeper than eared seals. True seals propel themselves forward with their back flippers and use their front flippers for steering and balance.

Most pinnipeds live in cool parts of the world, but a few live closer to the equator. You will learn more about fifteen species of pinnipeds in this book.

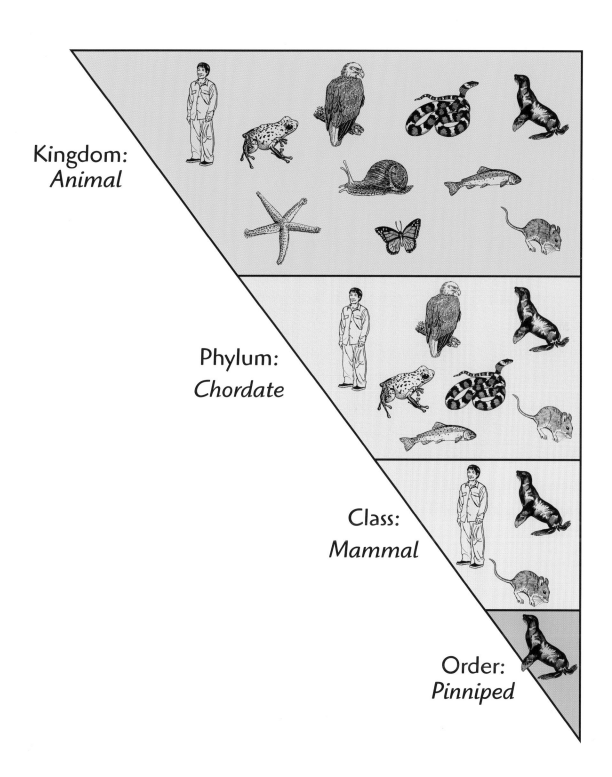

Kingdom: *Animal*

Phylum: *Chordate*

Class: *Mammal*

Order: *Pinniped*

Northern Seals

FAMILY: Phocidae

COMMON EXAMPLE: Baikal seal

GENUS AND SPECIES: *Phoca sibirica*

SIZE: 3 1/3 to 4 1/3 feet (1.1 to 1.3 m); up to 285 pounds (129 kg)

Baikal seals are the only pinnipeds that spend all their time in freshwater. They live in Lake Baikal and nearby rivers in Russia. No lake in the world is older, deeper, or is home to more kinds of plants and animals.

During the cold winter, Baikal seals stay below the ice most of the time. How do they breathe air below the ice? They keep small holes open to the surface. In February or March, females haul themselves up out of the water onto the ice and build a den in the snow that has built up on the ice. Then they give birth to babies. The newborns have long, white woolly fur. Soon they lose their fur and grow a new silvery gray coat.

Females usually nurse their pups for about 2 months. Then they choose a male and mate in the water. The males do not defend their territories, and they do not fight with one another.

Baikal seals molt on the ice in the spring. In warm years, they finish growing their new coat on land. These seals also spend time on shore during the summer. When they are on land, the seals must watch for their major *predator*—brown bears.

Baikal seals feed mostly at night. They make many short, shallow dives and eat a variety of fish. Although these seals spend most of their time alone, small groups may form when the fishing is good in one spot.

Northern Seals

FAMILY: Phocidae

COMMON EXAMPLE: Bearded seal

GENUS AND SPECIES: *Erignathus barbatus*

SIZE: 6 1/2 to 8 1/2 feet (2 to 2.6 m); up to
790 pounds (358 kg)

A bearded seal swims slowly, hovering just inches above the seafloor. Below its chin hang long, coarse, white whiskers that brush against the muddy bottom. The seal is searching for food—crabs, clams, and other shellfish—buried in the mud. When the seal feels a tasty treat, it uses the large claws on its front flippers to dig for its dinner.

Bearded seals live along the shallow coasts of the Arctic Ocean. They prefer waters sprinkled with drifting *ice floes*, but they also live in waters completely covered with thick sheets of ice. They travel long distances throughout the year. They follow the edge of the ice as it melts in the summer and then freezes in the winter.

Bearded seals spend most of their time alone, but they form small groups during the breeding season. Pups are born from March to May and can swim almost immediately. Females nurse their pups for less than 3 weeks, so the babies must gain weight quickly. The fatter pups are more likely to survive when their mothers leave.

These seals haul out onto the ice to molt, but they always stay close to the water. That way they can make a quick escape if they spot a hungry polar bear.

Northern Seals

FAMILY: Phocidae

COMMON EXAMPLE: Harbor seal

GENUS AND SPECIES: *Phoca vitulina*

SIZE: Males 5 to 6 1/2 feet (1.5 to 2 m); up to 375 pounds (170 kg)

Females 4 to 5 feet (1.2 to 1.5 m); up to 330 pounds (150 kg)

Harbor seals are common on both coasts of North America, northern Europe, and northeastern Asia. These seals stay close to shore, so people often notice large groups of them sunning themselves on rocky beaches.

Unlike their close relatives, the harp seals, harbor seals do not *migrate*. In fact, they usually travel no more than 10 miles (16 km) from the place they were born.

Newborn harbor seals can crawl and swim almost immediately. They nurse for 3 to 6 weeks on land or in the water. When a female feeds her pup, she leaves the baby for short periods of time to hunt in the ocean. Then she leaves her pudgy pup behind and chooses a male. When the harbor seals have mated, both head out to sea in search of food.

Although harbor seals have trouble moving on land, they come out of the water to rest and molt. Hauling out during molting warms their skin and makes the new fur grow in faster.

Harbor seals hunt a variety of fish and other small sea creatures. These seals may dive as deep as 1,640 feet (500 m) in search of food, and they may stay underwater for as long as 25 minutes. Because these seals eat some of the same species of fish as humans, they sometimes get caught in fishing nets and drown.

Northern Seals

FAMILY: Phocidae

COMMON EXAMPLE: Harp seal

GENUS AND SPECIES: *Phoca groenlandica*

SIZE: Males 5 1/2 to 6 1/4 feet (1.7 to 1.9 m); up to
300 pounds (136 kg)
Females 5 1/2 to 6 feet (1.7 to 1.8 m); up to
265 pounds (120 kg)

How did the harp seal get its name? An adult harp seal is gray with a
large, dark marking on its back and sides. Some people think that
this marking is shaped like the musical instrument. Other people say
it looks more like a horseshoe.

Harp seal pups are easily among the cutest babies in the world.
Newborns have pure white fur, large round eyes, and a dark snout.
They nurse for only about 2 weeks, but they often gain more than
7 pounds (3 kg) a day. After the female mates, she heads out to sea
and leaves her pup behind on the ice. Like other young seals, a harp
seal pup must learn to swim and hunt on its own.

Meanwhile, the female harp seal migrates north in search of food.
She must gain weight before April—when she will spend about a
month molting. When her brand new coat of fur has grown in, the
seal will continue her journey north, eating fish and other small sea
creatures. In late autumn, she will return to her winter *breeding
grounds* off the coast of Newfoundland, Canada.

Northern Seals

FAMILY: Phocidae

COMMON EXAMPLE: Hooded seal

GENUS AND SPECIES: *Cystophora cristata*

SIZE: Males 8 1/4 to 8 3/4 feet (2.5 to 2.7 m); up to 880 pounds (399 kg)

Females 6 1/2 to 7 1/4 feet (2 to 2.2 m); up to 660 pounds (299 kg)

It is early April in the North Atlantic. A newborn hooded seal pup nudges its mother's massive body. It is hungry. The female rolls on her side, and the baby eagerly takes a long drink of the richest milk in the world. After a 10-minute meal, the pup stretches, yawns, and falls asleep. Half an hour later, the pup wakes up and feeds some more. For the next 4 days, the pup will grow quickly and store up as much energy as it can.

As the female cares for her pup, several males watch her. They know that soon she will be ready to mate. When she is ready to leave the pup, two strong males swing into action. Each one inflates the black pouch that hangs over his snout and forehead. When the pouch, or hood, is fully expanded, it can be as large as two footballs. One male also blows up his bright red soccer ball-sized nostril sac and shakes it.

The males growl and lunge toward one another. One seal grabs the other by the neck and tears his rival's flesh. The wounded male slowly backs away. He knows he has been defeated.

After the victorious male and the female mate, they go their separate ways to gorge themselves on fish, squid, octopuses, and mussels. In the summer, large groups of hooded seals gather to molt. Then they continue their long journey in search of food until it is time to return to their breeding grounds.

Southern Seals

FAMILY: Phocidae
COMMON EXAMPLE: Northern elephant seal
GENUS AND SPECIES: *Mirounga angustirostris*
SIZE: Males 13 to 14 3/4 feet (4 to 4.5 m); up to
5,950 pounds (2,699 kg)
Females 6 1/2 to 9 3/4 feet (2 to 3 m); up to
1,985 pounds (900 kg)

One look at this seal and you'll know how it got its name. A male elephant seal has a large snout with a long flabby tip that looks something like an elephant's trunk. To attract mates and challenge rivals, the males inflate their special snouts and make calls that can be heard several miles away. Some people say these calls sound like someone blowing across the top of a gigantic empty glass soda bottle. Imagine that!

Each December, males arrive at their breeding grounds on small islands off the coasts of California and Mexico. The females arrive about a month later. They give birth to pups and spend about a month nursing them. When a pup is almost ready to survive on its own, its mother chooses a new mate.

The competition for females is fierce. Male elephant seals may look like blobs of bulging blubber, but they can charge with lightning speed. They also hack and slash at one another with their sharp teeth. Males have thick skin on their chest, so these battles are rarely fatal.

While the adults are on land, they do not eat at all. By the time they return to the water, males may have lost as much as 1,985 pounds (900 kg) and females may have lost 880 pounds (399 kg). They head for rich feeding grounds in the North. After eating plenty of squid, octopuses, sharks, rays, fish, and crabs, they return south to molt. Then they swim north and feed until it is time to breed again. No other mammal migrates twice a year.

Northern Seals

FAMILY: Phocidae
COMMON EXAMPLE: Ringed seal
GENUS AND SPECIES: *Phoca hispida*
SIZE: 3 3/4 to 4 1/2 feet (1.1 to 1.4 m); 110 to
310 pounds (50 to 141 kg)

Most adult ringed seals have gray coats covered with dark splotches that are surrounded by light-colored rings. They spend most of their time under ice-covered bays and *fjords* in the cold North. These seals usually live alone or in small groups.

In autumn, when openings in the ice begin freezing over, ringed seals punch breathing holes in the ice. These holes are shaped like an ice cream cone with the small end at the surface. During the winter, ringed seals keep the holes open with their strong claws.

In winter and early spring, ringed seals dig long, low dens in the snowdrifts above their breathing holes. A large hole at one end of each den acts as a doorway to the sea. The dens are safe, cozy places to escape from the bitter cold weather and hide from hungry predators. Males often rest in their dens, but females use them for another purpose. A den is the perfect place to give birth to a pup and nurse it.

Ringed seals molt on top of the ice in the early summer. Because these seals do not eat while they are molting, they lose a lot of weight. During the rest of the year, they eat fish, squid, and a variety of small ocean creatures.

Southern Seals

FAMILY: Phocidae
COMMON EXAMPLE: Weddell seal
GENUS AND SPECIES: *Leptonychotes weddellii*
SIZE: 8 1/4 feet (2.5 m); up to 990 pounds (449 kg)

In the early 1800s, a seal hunter named Captain James Weddell became the first European to observe a group of seals with long bodies and small heads. Since then, Weddell seals have been spotted on many southern islands, including Antarctica. They live closer to the South Pole than any other kind of seal.

Weddell seals eat fish, octopuses, and squid. To catch their *prey*, these seals commonly dive 650 to 1,310 feet (198 to 399 m) and stay underwater for about 15 minutes. These champion divers can go as deep as 1,970 feet (600 m) and stay underwater for as long as 73 minutes. They often fish for several hours and then rest for a few hours.

These seals spend the winter under the ice. Believe it or not, the chilly seawater is warmer than the freezing Antarctic air. How do Weddell seals breathe under the ice? They use their teeth to keep their breathing holes open. They also hunt for air pockets between the surface of the water and the ice. Here, they are relatively safe from their major predator—the killer whale.

Like other true seals, Weddell seals cannot walk across the ice. They use their sharp claws to drag their huge bodies wherever they need to go.

Fur Seals

FAMILY: Otariidae

COMMON EXAMPLE: Antarctic fur seal

GENUS AND SPECIES: *Arctocephalus gazella*

SIZE: Males 5 1/2 to 6 feet (1.7 to 1.8 m); up to 350 pounds (159 kg)

Females 3 3/4 to 4 feet (1.1 to 1.2 m); up to 112 pounds (51 kg)

In November, male Antarctic fur seals begin to arrive on the island of South Georgia and claim breeding territories. As more males come ashore, fights break out. The largest, strongest males end up with the best spots—the ones closest to the water. Soon the females arrive and give birth to the pups that have been growing inside them since last year's mating season.

A female stays with her pup and nurses it for about a week. Then she chooses a male, mates with him, and goes out to sea to hunt for food. A few days later, she returns to her pup and nurses it for a day or two. For the next few months, the mother continues this cycle. She nurses for a few days and then hunts, nurses and hunts, nurses and hunts.

Antarctic fur seals usually feed at night. Their main source of food is krill, a small shrimplike creature. They also eat fish, squid, and birds. Most of the time, they dive no deeper than 100 feet (30 m) and stay underwater for only a few minutes.

28

These seals were discovered in the late 1700s. For many years, hunters would search for their *rookeries* and slaughter the Antarctic fur seals as they slept. By 1900, only a few of these pinnipeds were left. Today there are laws to protect these seals. Scientists think that there are now more than a million Antarctic fur seals worldwide.

Sea Lions

FAMILY: Otariidae

COMMON EXAMPLE: California sea lion

GENUS AND SPECIES: *Zalophus californianus*

SIZE: Males 6 1/2 to 8 1/4 feet (2 to 2.5 m); up to 880 pounds (399 kg)

Females 5 to 6 1/2 feet (1.5 to 2 m); up to 240 pounds (109 kg)

It is early July. A large group of California sea lion pups wanders around a sandy beach. They play games like follow-the-leader, toss-the-seaweed, and throw-the-fish. After playing for a few hours, they plop down and take a nap.

When a female sea lion comes up on shore, she barks loudly. Her baby recognizes her call and answers with a tiny lamblike bleat. Mother and pup continue to call until they find one another. When they are close enough to touch, the sea lions sniff and touch noses. The mother rolls on her back, and the hungry pup takes a long drink of its mother's milk.

After a pup is born, its mother stays with it for about a week. Then she heads out to sea for a fishing trip that can last up to 3 days. When she returns, she feeds her pup for another few days then searches for more fish. This cycle usually lasts about 6 months.

As the females nurse their pups, the males are eagerly waiting to mate. They arrived at the breeding grounds before the females and have been defending territories for weeks. When the males fight, they push and shove one another. They even bite and slash rivals with their teeth. A female does not choose a mate until about a month after her pup is born.

After mating, males swim north to richer feeding grounds. Females do not migrate. They stay near the rookery all year long.

Fur Seals

FAMILY: Otariidae
COMMON EXAMPLE: Galapagos fur seal
GENUS AND SPECIES: *Arctocephalus galapagoensis*
SIZE: Males 5 feet (1.5 m); up to 141 pounds (64 kg)
           Females 4 feet (1.2 m); up to 60 pounds (27 kg)

Like other pinnipeds, Galapagos fur seals are meat-eaters. They spend a large part of their lives hunting for fish, squid, octopuses, and a variety of small ocean creatures. They usually make short, shallow dives no deeper than 66 feet (20 m). While they are underwater, they use their super-sensitive whiskers to find fish and avoid large objects, such as rocks.

You use your teeth to chew your food, but Galapagos fur seals and other pinnipeds usually swallow their food whole. They use their sharp, pointed teeth to grab and tear prey. If a seal catches a large animal, it shakes the prey until it breaks into smaller pieces.

Galapagos fur seals live in the Galapagos Islands, off the coast of Ecuador. They give birth and mate on rocky shores with sea caves, and they never travel too far from their breeding grounds.

These seals are the smallest pinnipeds, and they nurse their young for the longest period of time. Most pups drink their mothers' milk for 1 or 2 years, but sometimes even 3 year olds take an occasional drink of milk. The young begin to eat fish when they are about 9 months old.

Fur Seals

FAMILY: Otariidae

COMMON EXAMPLE: Northern fur seal

GENUS AND SPECIES: *Callorhinus ursinus*

SIZE: Males 7 feet (2.1 m); up to 600 pounds (272 kg)
Females 4 1/2 feet (1.4 m); up to 110 pounds
(50 kg)

In late June, a female northern fur seal arrives at St. Paul, a small island off the coast of Alaska. She struggles up the crowded beach, chooses a spot, and plops her heavy body in the sand. Less than a day later, she gives birth to a 12-pound (5.4-kg) pup.

The newborn spends most of its time drinking its mother's milk and sleeping. Less than a week later, the female chooses a male and mates. After a few more days, she leaves her pup to feed at sea. Like other eared seals, she spends the next few months feeding her pup onshore and hunting for fish and squid in the ocean.

Northern fur seals usually feed at night. During the day, they rest or travel. A 65-pound (29-kg) female may eat up to 9 pounds (4 kg) of fish each night. These seals usually dive down 223 feet (68 m) and stay underwater for about 3 minutes.

Although northern fur seals never swim far out to sea, they spend most of the year in the water. They migrate thousands of miles between their breeding grounds and their winter homes along the Pacific coasts of Canada, the United States, Russia, and Japan.

Fur Seals

FAMILY: Otariidae

COMMON EXAMPLE: South American fur seal

GENUS AND SPECIES: *Arctocephalus australis*

SIZE: Males 6 1/4 feet (1.9 m); up to 440 pounds (200 kg)
Females 4 3/4 feet (1.4 m); up to 132 pounds (60 kg)

It is early November. After months of fishing, a female South American fur seal heads toward the shore. A few days later, she gives birth to a healthy 11-pound (5-kg) pup. Almost immediately, she begins to nurse her baby with nutritious mother's milk.

About a week later, the female returns to the sea. She is so hungry that all she thinks about is a tasty meal of fish or sea snails. A killer whale is swimming nearby, but she doesn't notice it. A moment later, the mighty whale charges toward her at full speed. She spots her predator just in the nick of time and darts out of the whale's path. A frightened fur seal can swim up to 10 miles (16 km) an hour for a short distance.

Many pinnipeds live in the coldest parts of the world. The thick layer of blubber below their skin helps protect them from the freezing air and chilly water. South American fur seals live along the rocky coasts of Brazil, Argentina, Uruguay, Chile, Peru, and the Falkland Islands. The bright summer sun heats up the beaches where these seals breed and molt.

To stay cool, these fur seals spend much of their time in the ocean. The males fight bloody battles for territories that are under-water during high tide. Even though fur seal mothers nurse their pups on high, dry ground, they must make regular trips to the water to feed themselves.

Sea Lions

FAMILY: Otariidae

COMMON EXAMPLE: Steller sea lion

GENUS AND SPECIES: *Eumetopias jubatus*

SIZE: Males 10 feet (3 m); up to 2,200 pounds (998 kg)
Females 7 3/4 feet (2.4 m); up to 595 pounds
(270 kg)

In 1742, a scientist named Georg Wilhelm Steller wrote about a new group of sea lions that lives along the Pacific coast of North America. He had no trouble telling the difference between the males and females. The males are much larger and have a thick, strong neck with a long, shaggy mane. When they are upset, they roar like lions. This is how the Steller sea lion got its name.

This amazing animal glides through the water, rides high atop waves, and leaps up onto rocky ledges. To power its body forward, the Steller sea lion pulls its large front flippers in and then pushes them down. At the same time, the sea lion uses its back flippers to steer and keep its balance.

Each May, the males come ashore and claim breeding territories. A few weeks later, the females arrive and give birth. When the pups are born, they are dark brown to black and usually weigh from 35 to 50 pounds (16 to 23 kg). A Steller pup can walk almost immediately. Soon it learns how to scratch and groom its thick, dark brown coat with the three sharp nails on its flippers.

Newborns often have to wait their turn for their first milky meal. A female Steller sea lion often nurses her young for more than a year, so the new baby may have to compete with a 1 year old.

Walruses

FAMILY: Odobenidae

COMMON NAME: Walrus

GENUS AND SPECIES: *Odobenus rosmarus*

SIZE: Males 8 3/4 to 11 1/2 feet (2.7 to 3.5 m); up to 2,670 pounds (1,211 kg)

Females 7 1/3 to 10 1/4 feet (2.2 to 3.1 m); up to 1,835 pounds (832 kg)

The walrus's scientific name means "tooth-walking horse of the sea." That's a good way to describe this huge, tusk-towing creature. A walrus's ivory tusks are long, thick teeth that grow out of its upper jaw. They may be up to 22 inches (56 cm) long and 10 inches (25 cm) around. A female's tusks are slimmer, shorter, and more curved than a male's. Walruses use their tusks to pull themselves out of the water onto the ice, fight off polar bears, and defend their breeding territories.

As a walrus slowly glides along the ocean floor in search of clams, crabs, sea stars, and shrimp, its whiskers and tusks brush against the muddy bottom. When the walrus feels some prey, it digs down, sucks the animal out of its shell, and spits the empty shell back into the sea. A walrus may eat as much as 100 pounds (45 kg) of food a day.

What color is a walrus? That depends. When a walrus comes out of chilly ocean water, it looks grayish brown. But as it heats up, a walrus turns bright red. It isn't getting a sunburn, though. When the animal is in the water, it closes off blood vessels near its skin. This helps the walrus stay warm. When a walrus needs to cool down, it opens the blood vessels. As blood flows near the surface of its skin, heat escapes from the animal's body.

Amazing Facts About Pinnipeds

• Female hooded seals nurse their pups for only 4 days. These babies have the shortest nursing period of any mammal. A hooded seal's milk is eighteen times richer than a cow's milk. While nursing, hooded seal pups gain up to 15 pounds (7 kg) a day. At the same time, the female loses about 22 pounds (10 kg) a day.

• A Weddell seal has about two and a half times more blood than a person of the same size. These pinnipeds carry huge quantities of oxygen in their blood and muscles. All that oxygen comes in handy when they are diving for food.

• California sea lions often ride on the crests of waves, leap over breakers just before they crash, and jump through the air like dolphins. These pinnipeds are often trained to perform in shows at zoos, aquariums, and marine parks.

• During the 1700s and 1800s, European and North American hunters killed millions of pinnipeds. The animals' skins, meat, and the oil from their blubber were very valuable. Before electricity was invented, people used oil from seals and whales as fuel in lamps. Hunters preferred to hunt walruses and seals that gather in large groups because they could kill many animals in a short period of time.

Between 1810 and 1860, hunters killed about 250,000 northern elephant seals. By 1890, scientists thought all these pinnipeds had been killed. In the late 1890s, a few were discovered on a remote island owned by Mexico. The Mexican government posted soldiers on the island to protect the seals. Today there are as many northern elephant seals as there were before the hunting began. Other populations of pinnipeds are also recovering.

• Sharks and killer whales hunt many kinds of pinnipeds, but a pinniped's greatest enemy is humans. Each year, thousands of these marine mammals get tangled in fishing nets and drown. They are also threatened by pollution. Some choke on oil that has spilled out of big tankers. Others come into contact with chemicals that make it difficult for them to produce healthy young.

Words to Know

breeding ground—the place where pinnipeds go to mate and give birth to young

breeding season—the time of year when pinnipeds mate and give birth to young

class—a group of creatures within a phylum that shares certain characteristics

family—a group of creatures within an order that shares certain characteristics

fjord—a narrow ocean passage between cliffs or steep slopes

genus (plural **genera**)—a group of creatures within a family that shares certain characteristics

ice floe—a large sheet of ice floating in a large body of water

kingdom—one of the five divisions into which all living things are placed: the animal kingdom, the plant kingdom, the fungus kingdom, the moneran kingdom, and the protist kingdom

mammal—an animal that has a backbone and drinks mother's milk when it is young

migrate—to travel to find food or a mate

molt—to shed an old layer of skin or fur and grow a new one

order—a group of creatures within a class that shares certain characteristics

oxygen—an important chemical needed for life and found in the air

phylum (plural **phyla**)—a group of creatures within a kingdom that shares certain characteristics

pinniped—an order of marine mammals that have flippers and divide their time between the ocean and the land

predator—an animal that hunts and eats other animals

prey—an animal that is hunted and eaten by other animals

rookery—the place where large groups of animals gather to give birth and raise their young. For many pinnipeds, the same area of land or ice serves as their rookery and breeding grounds.

species—a group of creatures within a genus that shares certain characteristics. Members of a species can mate and produce young.

territory—the area of land that an animal claims as its own and defends against rivals

Learning More

Books

Davis, Deborah. *The Secret of the Seal*. New York: Random House, 1994.

Hodge, Judith Walker. *Seals, Sea Lions, and Walruses*. Hauppauge, NY: Barrons, 1999.

Knudtson, Peter. *The World of Walrus*. Boston: Sierra Club Books, 1998.

Matthew, Downs. *Harp Seal Pups*. New York: Simon & Schuster, 1997.

Miller, David. *Seals and Sea Lions*. New York: Voyageur Press, 1998.

Staub, Frank J. *Sea Lions*. Minneapolis, MN: Lerner, 2000.

Woodward, John. *Endangered Seals*. New York: Benchmark Books, 1997.

Web Sites

Seal Conservation Society
http://www.greenchannel.com/tec/species/species.htm
See all thirty-three species of pinnipeds at this site. Brief descriptions of each one provide information about their physical appearance and lifestyle.

Walrus
http://www.seaworld.org/walrus/walrus.html
This site was developed and is maintained by Seaworld Marine Parks. It features a variety of interesting facts about walruses.

Index

About the Author

Melissa Stewart's fascination with pinnipeds began when she swam with sea lions off the coast of Floreana, one of the Galapagos Islands. She was mesmerized as the large, graceful creatures flowed effortlessly through water that chilled her to the bone. The sea lions dove down, spun in circles, and twisted their bodies this way and that. One fearless sea lion darted toward her at top speed and then turned away just in the nick of time. It just wanted to play.

Ms. Stewart has degrees in biology and science journalism, and has been writing about science, nature, and health for more than a decade. She has written eight children's books and numerous articles for magazines and newspapers. Ms. Stewart lives in Marlborough, Massachusetts.